just living

just living

William Robertson

COTEAU
BOOKS

Edited by Geoffrey Ursell.
Cover and book design by Duncan Campbell.
Cover image, "Father and Baby at Breakfast" by Veronique Decruck P / Getty Images.
Printed and bound in Canada at Marc Veilleux Imprimeur Inc.

Library and Archives Canada Cataloguing in Publication

Robertson, William B., 1954-
    Just living / William Robertson.

Poems.
ISBN-13: 978-1-55050-320-3
ISBN-10: 1-55050-320-0

    I. Title.

PS8585.O322J88 2005   C811'.54   C2005-905080-2

1 2 3 4 5 6 7 8 9 10

COTEAU
BOOKS

2517 Victoria Avenue
Regina, Saskatchewan
Canada   S4P 0T2

Available in Canada and the US from:
Fitzhenry & Whiteside
195 Allstate Parkway
Markham, Ontario
Canada   L3R 4T8

The publisher gratefully acknowledges the financial assistance of the Saskatchewan Arts Board, the Canada Council for the Arts, the Government of Canada through the Book Publishing Industry Development Program (BPIDP), the Government of Saskatchewan, through the Cultural Industries Development Fund, and the City of Regina Arts Commission, for its publishing program.

For Mary

Contents:

One: Sabotage

Two:Stormy Weather

Three: My Home With You

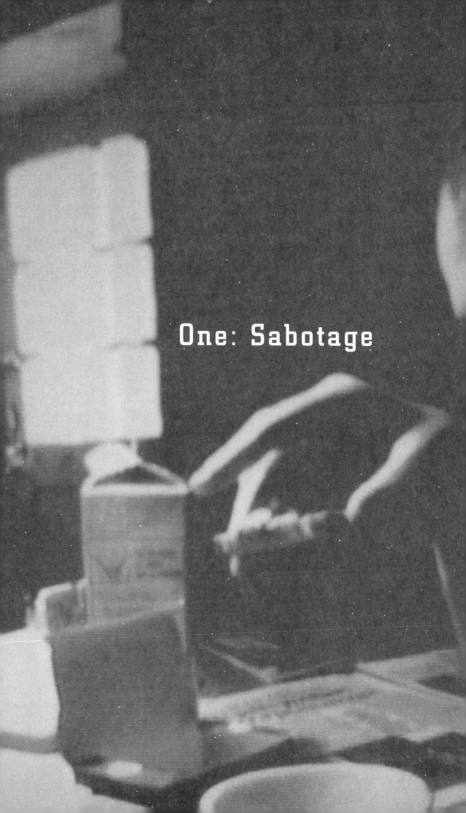

One: Sabotage

Grain Prices

My old best friend and I,
my boozing buddy
with whom I shared
the front seat of a Pontiac
and barrooms all over
Texas and our hometown,
are talking seriously right now
for the first time in years
about inland grain terminals, the threat
to the farmer, the quality of last fall's
crop in southwest Saskatchewan
when his wife walks in
to remind him my life
is falling apart, that's why
I'm here, then turns
back to the kitchen.

We stare at each other.

I remember one night
in Lubbock, Texas
the car ride was long, the beer
many and cold.
                We talked about home,
about women, but
I think we'll stick
with grain prices for now.

Talking It Over

While I shovel the walk
   I talk to my wife
do the laundry
   I talk to my lover

drive the car
   explain to the kids
look for my friend
   he's got kids of his own

talk to my parents
   they give me advice
talk to the doctor
   he says that's a hard choice

talk to my wife
   she says I'm your lover
talk to my lover
   she says I'm not your wife

talk to my kids
   they say where's supper
talk to the liquor?
   it's over for me

crawl into bed
   argue with God
get up for a walk
   and listen to the stars

Even Blues

When I leave her arms I bound
back to my life buoyant, put on
ram-hard rock music, wild around
my kitchen waving the serrated knife.

By late evening supper's over
dishes done, kids to bed
can't believe who that guy in the kitchen was
put on Mozart, hold my head.

Four a.m. I'm alert and empty
a head full of jagged notes
one line from a love song teasing me
insomniac hope.

Two days go by without her
music's something other people play
don't want any female folk music, be-
bop, even blues to mess such a blue day.

Force

If you called now

when my wife is on the couch
with our youngest, reading a story,
our oldest is doing dishes, whistling,
like supper was a breeze
after the hours his parents spent
hushed in their bedroom,
and the light is carefully golden
the house warm, the flowers
my wife bought me wink happily
on the table, the card says All
My Love, and the man it's addressed to
sits here stiff in his chair
surveying the house and books
he thought he'd own forever

you might just bring the whole place
down.

Punishment

Yesterday I missed the bathroom doorway,
smashed into the wall.
I've done that
four times now.
My shin still hurts
where I dropped the drinking glass
three days ago.
My body's so stupid
it can't do anything right
anymore, lifts its head
into cupboards, trips on stairs,
exhausts itself every night
on a bed of sweat.

This is what you get
for loving outside
your home.

I used to be safe here,
spent long days all alone
practising for people
to come through.
Like all the best performances
mine were private. Pirouetted
round the kitchen with sharp knives:
never a drop of blood.
Sprinted two flights of stairs
with a laundry basket:
never a broken bone.
God I was good.

Now I've gone bad.
Stupid body aching

for love, hurting itself
for something it shouldn't
have.

Embrace

Because your golden bracelet smoothed up and down your slender wrist, forearm to hand that I would hold and kiss

Because your green dress measured softly those places I would take my tongue, my fingers, the long lean inside of my leg

Because your flat brown shoes looked so easy to undo, kick aside next to my undone shoes, so you could run your toes along my arch, watch me rise from your rug, ebb again across that floor

Because of the scent, something of flowers I caught when passing behind your chair, a scent that could saturate the weave of cloth, my suit hanging hungry in my closet

These things so light and easy on you, the distance between us so thick with clothes and ties and shoes, so chatter-full to fill the guest book of others' love I read at the side of the room while the bride and groom went round, bare hand in bare so-promising hand, their eyes alive with assurance

Because of all these things, let me tell you how tightly I hold still the quiet moment in the doorway of that church basement linoleum place, your two fingers, my one, clasped for a perfect instant, no one around us as our daring careful fingers performed our best, our fullest embrace

All Smiles

I'm sitting in a room full of pictures.
My parents have us all over their walls
proud graduates with mortars and scrolls,
sisters in wedding gowns, their babies.

In one my family surrounds me,
two-year-old on my lap. I remember
the day it was taken, forcing the kids
into good clothes and smiles up against
our piano for the homey look. The photographer
didn't catch my bottle of beer –
three in the afternoon, the guy
and my wife turned down repeated requests
to join me in a drink. My smile
tacked now to my parents' wall, my first
graduation portrait, a boy with contact lenses
peeled that morning from the bathroom floor,
hands shaking so badly they could hardly
find my eyes, red and scared of something
up there above me with my sisters'
happy kids.

Holy Orders

In tonight's movie about nuns my mother
cries because it's inspirational
I cry because I miss you, keep
seeing you in a black and white
habit, my mood smiling
one second, emptied the next
thinking back to the time we walked
through the grounds of the convent
you told me after all the pain
of lack of love and looking,
Jesus, looking, you'd even considered
taking the veil and leaving
us all behind, thinking you'd
find a way of living without
some decent upright man who couldn't
just shake loose and love you.

Aren't movies easy: look
at my mother crying for love
of the good thing and seeing,
possibly, herself. I see
you, quiet and loved, no more acting
gentle and serene, and me
nowhere but here in this chair,
the audience,
alone, and watching.

Bare Essentials

When I leave your house so full
of you I could howl
to shake each home
I own this city, every stick
of wood and chunk of concrete
but I'd give it all away
every yard of it and sprinklers
hissing in the dark
just leave me that room where we
stretched the walls tonight.

Waltzing down your street
and across main drag
I own this strip of light
this low rumble of motors
and curvy chassis teenaged girls
calling at me out their windows
but I'd give them all away
give 'em to this rumble of boys
bearing down behind
watching me watch them with their
scared brutal eyes
just give me that glint
of penny shining
new in the dirt
what I've wished for
what I've got tonight.

Rubbing my face in the dark
of my yard I smell you
on my hands, each eager finger
so wild with you I could swallow
the sky, but I'll leave it
for the next guy, just leave me

that slip of moon
to hang my coat on
while I lay me
so slow floating down so free
to sleep.

She Visits Victoria

Down at the ocean's side she can
say anything she wants
about her lover's eyes and no salt
no gull no freighter far out there
heading maybe for Japan
will care or misunderstand
what it was she said and why
she's come here to say it.
His hair, the bumps of his ribs,
the way, when he's on the telephone,
he says her name so low it feels
as if he's found every place
she's ever kept secret, even
from those she'd meant to share
the world with – and now alone
on this pebble-tossed shore she tells
a trawler she's finding smooth stones
for his hands, shells to lay across
his chest, cedar to smell, bits
of coloured glass he can look through
when he says her name low
as the murmur of salt-
water waves.

Patience

Neatly into my glove
fits the smooth green stone my
lover brought from the seaside
for me to hold

into the wind-crusted snow
of southwest Saskatchewan,
my father beside me
trying his best to explain
how to love a woman, perhaps
let another go,
the seventy-year-old minister
standing dumbfounded,
even angry, before his son
at the end of all he knows.

My mother, a minister's daughter,
waits for us at home
wanting hard to take my problems
make them small, make them
her own, their son
in the doorway cold

still holding hard
the stone she gave him
smooth piece of herself
exquisite and free
of solutions.

In the Snow

When the roast burned black
and smoked the kitchen
she pitched it, pot and all,
into the clean backyard
where it hissed a hole in the snow.
Her father-in-law, roused momentarily
from the pre-game Super Bowl,
told his son he'd never
had to order out Sunday supper
in his life. His son said cautiously
there was that one time
and his father told him, again,
that's not the way it happened.

Returning to her room and notepaper
she continues writing a letter
to her father, tells him
the waxwings have returned,
that she walked for hours
with a man and found spring totems
in the snow: a stick of poplar
she broke and held to her nose
its musk pushing her into the man
how they fell at the side of the road
and rolled in thick quilts of winter clothes
the insulation unable to conceal from her
the feel of the man's own spring rising
or from him the gentle drifts
beneath her coat. Walking again she found
maple propellers, fairy wings she calls them,
threw them high and cheered. Sticks and seedlings,
a man hot in the snow, these things
she tries to write and ask
if her father knows

how to get through Super Bowl Sunday
when you've thrown out the roast,
how to get through all the football Sundays,
a man downstairs assuring his father
his wife's just fine and the old man
doesn't have to go.

Another man waiting silently
in the snow.

The Window Above Your Bed

I want to come to you like
the sound of ice releasing
this city to the splash
of tires, the sucking sound
of mud and children
kicking their way through
puddles, snow pants soaked,
everything coming loose
at once, basements damp,
sky blue, waxwings lisping
at soggy brown apples
outside your loamy window
no longer frozen you
can slide it open, pull me
through, hear the creak
of my bending, the moan
as I fall.

The Old Way

I call you angel, you
shudder away, say
no,
woman.

I try the other
old endearments
learned along the way:
sweetheart
from my parents
darling from a song
baby from all over
remember hating it
as a child, those silly
teenagers cooing, don't
worry baby, movie men
levelling it
like a gun: don't
worry baby. Now
I mouth it, mean it
but all the stuff
behind clangs in.
Even our names,
William and Mary,
blessed and bloodied
by long generations.

Seems we have to remake
these words with our world
but while the hair
you've just brushed back
about your head
catches the sun

all my old versions
of angel
attend
your face.

Touching Myself

Because the touch of her hand
along my face causes me
to shudder down unsteadily
into silence
Because she can't come and soothe
this tired troubled man,
her words on the phone
to calm myself, lie down in the semi-darkness
of my blinds-drawn room and touch
my face with a healing hand,
sound strange, like I have no right
to touch myself there
without a razor.

Be gentle with yourself she says
and I run my hand along my jaw
see my fingers on her face
the just-bristly feel of tiny golden hairs
on her upper lip. I touch my cheek bones
take the gentle shape of her eyes and nose
her throat that quivers so slightly
when I run my lips along it, my gentle
well-taught hands explore between the buttons
of my shirt, the explosion of hair,
the soft undergarments I'd touch
were she here and my hands there,
my fingers nudge beneath the line
of her belt, lift myself up
by the hardness she's felt till the bed
bucks me hard and a spray of stars
where her touch is my touch
her face
my face.

In Irish Poems

Remember the afternoon we went
a little crazy
you said you liked an Irish poet
I ran you to my bookshelf where
you looked and said I think I have one
you don't, then told me of a class
you took – your prize-winning essay
on Irish literature – I scrambled
to do one better, frantic to prove
my worth
           like the night we walked blocks on blocks
piling up stories of bad cheques,
criminal records, cruising the bars on Yonge
right in there, trying to match each other
going one better, one worse
warning each other:

    now will you still love me?
    now will you stop?

Now we're apart
I get reckless
flesh out
your seamiest stories
slam my fist
into my heart, never
think about the sunny day
we took one another's hands
and prayed:
        an open road
        a clear sky
        your shoulder strong
        against my arm.

Little Task

There, I've done it
climbed the steps
from my basement suite
to my landlady's back-door screen
mouthed your name
to the full moon
stars I couldn't see
trees that swayed
in the late August breeze
fruit hanging heavy
waiting, each apple, each plum
for your lips
red curves in the dark
and soft like your name
whispered into night
that last thing I had
to do
before bed.

How Hard to Kick
for Ron M.

For my friend caught
in the Australian riptide
salvation was a sixty-five-year-old
surfer a head shorter than him
made of sinew and old leather
His only words were "need
a hand?" and "kick like hell"
which they did
being as my friend
had just that morning decided
to live, come back
to his life and give
most of the things away
that dragged him down
to the point where he couldn't tell
a strong current from a wave
standing in an undertow
watching dolphins play

He tells me this story
walking his dog through snow
as an illustration of what to do
with the thousands of things
a lawyer can charge you
to count and divide
as if one's life was measured
by trays and fish plates
which it was
a house packed full of them
when all he needed,
says my friend,
was a wiry man
who knew the sea

to come and offer him
a piece of board
and teach him how hard
to kick

Messages

Taped to the wall above my table
a postcard: pueblo church
in New Mexico with two
wooden crosses.
The wall is pale green and the former
tenants have carved in their initials
or some attempt at words.
Why do people do things like that?
My drunken landlord probably
didn't even notice. He won't notice
if I steal a lamp. But I won't.
Just sit at the table and ponder
the latest words with my wife
how she retrieved our daughter's
belongings from the Y
full of dried bloody rags and notes
about slashing, the girl run to Vancouver
and working, she tells us, her mother
and I apart, both educated and no words
I can send about the room I'm in,
cuttings in the wall, a couple
of crosses on a postcard meaning
someone made a mistake, someone
supposedly died for my sake, for
the woman I walked away from
an hour ago, for this girl
we gave our name to, then let go.
The thin white lines on her wrists
are part of mystery to me
now. And the landlord's staggering,
the marks I leave on his wall.

Bopping

slow boogie woogie piano of nina simone's "my baby just cares for
me" in my landlord's living room signs of his imminent collapse
overflowing garbage cans beer cans coffee table unanswered letters
copies of newspaper articles about something he'd do something
about if he wasn't in hospital freeing up his turntable to nina little
girl blue in a jazz club with gentle hands on drums slow boogie
singing who her baby cares for telling me who my baby cares for
bopping my head to her telling me telling me while she dies we die
nina slowly helps me die my landlord's lonely disease

Charlie Parker Playing "My Old Flame"

There was nothing about the night that I'd call extraordinary. Just me sabotaging my marriage. I don't know what it was. I wasn't all that unhappy. I just needed something else, and she did too.

Her old man was a longshoreman, big as two of me, but he worked nights so he wasn't a problem. We always met at a bar or a club. Out-of-the-way places where we could be in a crowd.

But no crowd that night. Her and me, leaning together over a table against the wall, her not sure if she wants to leave her husband yet, and asking me what excuse I gave my wife tonight. Up against the bar a sailor and two guys in fedoras talking baseball with the bartender.

Over in the corner, on a little stage, some coloured guys playing jazz. Slow stuff, and her and me not getting anywhere, just putting in time away from home.

Then the men at the bar break up laughing, the two guys in hats throw down some bills and walk out the door. The sailor gets up and walks into the bathroom and the bartender comes around the end of the bar and asks can he get us another. She doesn't look at him so I say no and we get up to leave.

It was nothing doing with us that night. In the doorway of the bar when I told her I'd see her home she said I probably would. Now what can you do with that?

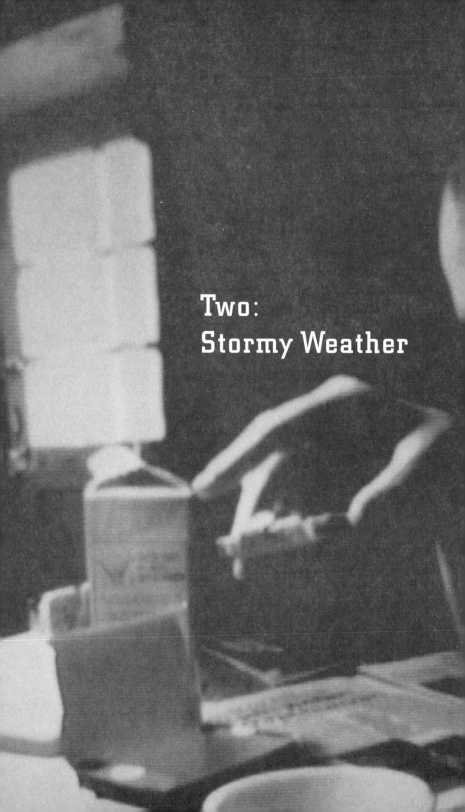

Two:
Stormy Weather

Showing Off

I remember the clowns in high school
who couldn't do a thing
without shouting "Hey Barbara,
look at me"
and whatever they did
they did well
and I hated them
but Barbara, well,
I couldn't hate her,
though she smiled at the clowns
bombing around town in their cars
with their heads on springs
in the windows

every summer they took over
the pool, lined up at the high board
to spring in beautiful arcs
across the eyes of the girls, alerted
with a "Yoo hoo, Louise,
Laverne, look here,"
and I watched, dripping
disgust.

Now, better late than never,
as they say,
I'm learning to dive
into swimming pools
hockey pools, who cares what pools
I've watched you
from across the room
for too long
and I'm ready to risk
making a fool of myself

with a high dive in the eye
of the sun

Are you watching me?

Here goes.

Begin Again

I want to love you
blindfolded, my devouring eyes
trained on bikinis and magazines,
think they know so much
take shortcuts every time
Tie me blind and take
your time, come to me slowly
(come from behind)
Let my hands discover
beneath your summer dress
the lightness it uses
to cover so much: the hips'
sweet flare, back
so straight, little
bulge of belly where
blind hands meet,
how my toes along your thighs
tighten your sinews to a quiver,
each ear's salty conch
eyelids' gentle covers,
I want to find you all over
again, tie me blind
please
take your time

Watch Her Work

They line the hall outside her office
getting ready to be shot, the same joke
over and over except for the one
woman who say's it'll be fun
to get something stuck into her
by a woman for a change.

The men all laugh as
if they find this funny
in line for the nurse
who doesn't look like a nurse,
long blue skirt with a slit
up the side, yellow blouse and sweater
I've just come to watch
for a minute. She studies each arm
through the glasses she wears in bed
when she reads beside me, sweater
in the closet, skirt on a hook.

All the employees nervily shuffling up
the hall while I just get to stand
and look at the way she takes
each arm, slides in the needle, presses
gently on each person a swab, a calm word
that makes them laugh and leave
for the next in line who's never
me, just taking a break
from my own job
to watch her work,
doling out these small
necessary hurts.

Your Hands

Your hands make me beautiful
stroking my belly, the hairs
on my chest, used to be I could
hardly get undressed in light
all the ugliness I'd cast upon myself
frightening me from the mirror
from the eyes of lovers
scared girls
who listened to me drink my way
through sad stories I was
the butt of, pushing women away
pushing me farther
into clothes I let you undo
so you can stroke me
changing my shape as you move
calling you beautiful beautiful
you closing my lips
such a struggle to shut up
a man who's confessed so many times
all his infirmities, calamities
the negligence he's allowed
this body, these thighs
never admitting they could
fill the eyes of someone who
loved them, running her hand
down them and behind
the knee, such freedom
to be the person I
hated so long I tried
to kill him the coward's way
such slow pain I want
to tell you about but
your fingers again
across my lips, your hands
urge all that's ugly
to silence.

Summer

She sits in the chair and cries
He has seen her do this before
and sometimes he goes to her
strokes her hair and tells her
good things, other times
she sends him away

What he wants, of course, is a signal
He's over halfway through his life
and at times thinks he knows things
but this woman new to him
has as much pain behind her as
he does. He doesn't know
which hurt goes with which line
on the face he loves
takes carefully in his hands
looks steadily through its windows
to a place where they move with ease

Some days she calls it summer
others it's the way they cross the floor
at dance class, their holiday from
the slow coldness winter puts on
everything, her stiff shoulders
heaving with tears she
sends down those cheeks he'd cup
in hands this winter has roughened
feels in a heart so many winters
have hardened, standing a few feet
                        behind her
waiting for the signal his heart
is still soft enough to learn.

The Invention of Vancouver

My daughter has recently invented
Vancouver, starting at the welfare office
working out past the shelter
to an apartment on East Georgia
she lays down buildings in the city
she created two years ago
snapping angrily at me about Saskatoon
its school its rules.

I remember then I told her
about Vancouver, the first Canadian city
I lived in after Japan: Richmond in 1959,
going for shots, how I wanted to be brave
told the nurse rather than cry
I'd howl like a wolf
and howled, as she stuck me again,
till I cried. Told the girl about
uncle Syd's hazelnut orchard
on Lulu Island, the ditches
full of water and little bridges
to cross them, how my father
one Saturday morning plunged his hand
into his pocket, retrieved a spread
of spangling change, the quarters I saw
had antlers, were all about
Canada and my daughter yawned.
She could tell I knew nothing
about Vancouver.

I tried her over and over: my visit in '64
the PNE in '66, hitchhiking through in '76.
In '79 I got thrown out of a bar
at Horsehoe Bay. My daughter stopped me
wanted to know was I physically

thrown out, I said yes, I got the true
bum's rush, my roommate following sheepishly
had to stop me down on the docks
from diving in naked at midnight
thinking I could swim to the ferry
lit up like a birthday cake
for someone famous – me – the returning
hero, famous for having lived here
famous for wanting badly to be somebody
even just a guy who'd swim drunk
and naked to the Nanaimo ferry
drown halfway and be some small
statistic in the Vancouver *SUN*
my roommate retrieving my scattered
clothes, not used to having to hold
and dress a man.
I told him as we drove out next day
By God, we showed 'em
and I'm sure he nodded, glad
to get away.

Your mother and I honeymooned
through in '82, I said, we ate
like we owned the place
I tried to show her a good time
spouting names like an old Vancouverite
ending up in the right place
by accident, I may only have impressed her
with my ability
to land on my feet.

Now my daughter's phoned me
after weeks of silence
says she's in Vancouver, I should
see the place, it's the answer
to her every prayer.
I can see her inventing that city
like you do when you're seventeen
every bus stops for you
every street bears your name
and every father who was ever
a boy who fucked up even once
can scatter fresh-minted quarters
gleaming across her path.

Stormy Weather

This is the summer the clouds
pile up at the end of every street
out of the city like mounds
of ice cream, great gobs
of new mountain ranges changing
shape overnight and through the day.
The summer the rain mystifies
everyone, here for an hour
and gone, flooded basements, washed-out
gardens, ball game cancellations
on radios crackling with light.
Then the winds move in
snapping off fifty-foot trees.
City crews work overtime
to clear the streets, the highway ditches
fill with water and tanker trucks
roll on their backs
like June bugs.

This is the summer of ants in every
basement, driven there by the water,
some say, of chemical sprays
and people who pooh-pooh the chemicals
saying just lay down whole cloves
and your ants will go. The summer
the ants crawl over the cloves.

This is the summer of the merlins,
pigeon hawks, skirling round
our heads like toy planes
rousting out songbirds
of the neighbourhood to be killed
for their babies. The university ornithologists
hush our talk about their incessant

shrieks, tell us they're endangered
species but that our city, proudly,
has a pair every so many
blocks, shattering the five a.m.
sky and tipping it in the window
over my bed.

This is the summer I take my son
to stay with my parents because
I can't afford to keep him.
His mother drives to the coast
to talk with her best friend, then
I take our son back to her but
first I take him round to Eastend
to see the dinosaur they've
dug up, lying there
in chunks the colour of the land
around it. We look over
the archaeologists' shoulders to try
and imagine its size shadowing us
suddenly with instant death, my son
a bit disappointed until he sees
the tooth sticking up from the rock,
just that. Six inches long and deadly.
All he needs
to reconstruct the summer.

Funny Guy

My son wants to be a funny guy
has been making up jokes for years
he imitates TV stars, older kids, and me
running lines and laughing while
he tells a story that someone laughed at
somewhere, all the way down the lake
and back in the canoe, sun hot above
nowhere to go but dig in with the paddle
while he laughs at how hard I'm working
how far we've got to go, he mis-casts his line
smacks me with the lure then laughs
while we stop and sort out hooks.
Get home and he hides my drink
hides my knife when I go to clean
his fish, looking me in the face each time
Is this funny, Dad? Are you
laughing yet? Each time having to say
No, those are my glasses you broke,
or my fishing rod. No, I'm tired, son,
want a cold drink and lunch made.
No, it's just you and me kid, on a lake
where the three of us used to go
but I left your mother and you're
a real kidder now, making a joke
of everything I do.

Forts

Riding home I'm surprised
by two boys yelling Hi
from their grass fort
silver pistols in hand
I've grown so old I thought
it only a pile of grass
so deep in argument
with my lover over kids
who aren't here, my lover
gone too, just me running
through the moves in a story
that's tired already, these boys
happy as a tenth birthday party
asking about my son, my bike,
giving me such warm diversion
I move way past them to climb
into a fort of boulders
at the edge of Camerons' field
a place I went alone with my
father's cigarettes, desperate to believe
this could be home.

The night such thoughts became obsession
I had friends tie me in the trees
promise not to tell and let
my parents find me, and they did,
and the fort in my closet, the one
behind the furnace, as well, we had a beauty
at the back of Halville schoolyard
the teachers had to kick in, so angry
we were, such accomplishment to build,
these boys with their pistols
and grassy-legged pants so happy
to show me what they've done

such a world to build away from
such stupid fights you can have
instead of nesting with a lover
who built forts as a girl

where she dreamed being big
and having kids she'd never
be angry with, a kind man
she'd call husband, a fort
they'd call home.

End of a Workday in Fall

Bring me your stories of women
who slap one another on the job
because one or the other's
husband got drunk and left
or stayed
the woman whose breast
was removed
the one whose son died
she showed up for work
the next day saying I can't
help it

String them out along
the riverbank in the gold
of this late October miracle
snowless and not cold

Interrupt yourself and point me
at heads of grass grabbing
little pieces of sun
falling fast behind the city's
shining buildings

Then freight each goose climbing
the late blue above
with the pain of women at work
watch them carry it
far across fields
then south
such pain, such gold.

Winter Coming

Cold November moon's a frosty white
thumbtack holding up a ragged
set of sheers scooting east
to Manitoba, the Rockies
sending us their snow
the sidewalk outside this café
bouncing back the fast footsteps
to a cold car, the seat I'm going
to have to get a blanket for
my bum so cold, yours so good
to hold when we get home
chattering cheerful curses
at a whole winter still
to come as we unwrap
the layers of clothes like Christmas
paper also yet to come, November
to be gotten through in shivers
beneath this blanket in our bedroom
where you rise in your smooth
white skin above me, surprising me again
like a child with snow
this warm blizzard of affection
I'm coming to know.

Winter Kiss

some few seconds of this cold
January morning as I go out
in the dark in unlaced boots
to start my cold complaining car
for the two-hour drive to work
she – in her housecoat and with half-closed
eyes – snatches my two boiled eggs
from the pot where they've cooled overnight
and draws on them a love message
I notice when I open my lunch
five hours later: just a heart
in blue ink and her initial

and doesn't that man wrapped
in his parka and grim determination
to get through another Saskatchewan
winter alive give me the oddest look
in through the window
as I – as far as he can tell –
kiss an egg, such an ordinary snow-
white thing I pull from my lunch bag
then touch my lips to her heart,
to her sweet blue strokes

Work

Forty-two below in Saskatoon
the car so cold it doesn't
want to go, but I force it
back into the ice-fog street
to join the cranky parade of others
with no options
but to work

the freeway's a sheet of ice
every other car a sliding weapon
as she sits beside me worried
what the day will do to her
sixth day on the job
the first where she goes it alone
house to house checking
bedsores, poking fingers for blood
sugar, lancing boils, trying to help
some poor four-hundred-pound woman clean
the folds of her huge
unhappiness, braving warnings
of weirdos who want to touch
her breast while she rewraps
the dressing on a gangrenous wound

I hear these stories later while we
get undressed, climb into the bed
so cold she wants to
hold me hard and hell
I'm only human, want to touch
the same place the weirdos at work did
and she lets me
examine the body that doesn't
need a doctor or nurse
to tell me it's healthy

and with a giggling curse
at the cold we'll later be so proud
to have lived through we roll
ourselves into a tight ball
of gratitude for work, this warm
place to go to
when it's over

Sun Celebration

In the hours before church
   and after sleep
I kneel at the shrine
   God's given you
   God's given me
from which a baby
perhaps a baby
     to be
touch my finger
to the waters
another finger
another finger
my hands opening you
your body opening me
each man another layer

each layer of shed man
shaken loose on white sheets
such trust in such touching
such touching so deep
cries like children

wet as newborns
wet as fishes
wet as lovers
shedding old skins
glistening new skins
Sunday morning
set ablaze

Moonwild

God loves a pair of drunken lovers
don't you know
                    even if drunk
only on moon   its lunatic pull
yanking us both   off balance
till we lean
                    into a curve
                              of fear
    afraid   almost   to love
this wildness racing our hearts

God watching all and saying
        I like this pair

let them lean hard
into their moonwild fear
let them love hard
at the dark

He Wakes Her

in the four a.m. black
his head back on the pillow
of the sturdy bed they bought
his lungs his mouth his yellow teeth
drag four jagged notes
from their mutual air
and she gets up on her elbow
to look at him
the gaping maw she can just
see, this man she may not
know at this dark moment
then he whimpers, twists shut
and she recognizes the lips
that lately sucked her glorious
breasts, his adjective
her everyday noun just
letting him come to her
shudder down into quiet
he tears open hours later
and she chuckles
at the sight of him returning
to himself
the ordinary sound he makes
just living

Three:
My Home with You

End of the '90s Poem

I'm sick of irony.

I love you.

Let's get married.

We'll wear nice clothes and invite
a few friends.

The wedding can be in a church.

Afterwards we can have a big supper
and a party.

Over the years we can use words
like husband and wife. My wife
bought that. My husband snores.

See how easy that is.

I meant every word I just said.

Language Lesson

Holding you in our kitchen
as the light shades away
into another hot night, we take off
our shirts, tempted by the discomfort
of rubbing sticky skin together,
take the water pitcher from the fridge
and pour tall glasses to rub
down the runnels of our spines
between your breasts
across our foreheads
clear, cold water.

Omizu we called it in Japan
when I was a little boy
Oh-me-zoo, the sound
winding its way around us
as you dip your fingers in your glass
and write imagined characters
on my chest, my stomach
what I was bathed in
after I was born
in the home my parents, young missionaries,
shared with their first child
and a maid, Tomiko San, who called it
omizu, who felt it on her fingers
and in her mouth as omizu.

What you repeat as you
pour out more, our stickiness
wiped away, renewed, wiped away
again. What do I remember
you ask, and I tell you what little
I know, how to count to ten, how
to say bathroom, a few other essentials,

and omizu, as we wash ourselves
for bed, one finger, one damp limb,
at a time.

So Healthy

Here it is one of our first
very hot summer days and you
so sick you can barely slump
over the kitchen table where I
feed you scones and marmalade
so well, so healthy, I can't
help feeling ashamed of myself
every time I catch sight
of your breasts down the front
of the loose blue summer housedress
you slept in last night, too sick
to pull it over your head you lay
with an arm flung out at me
and our third thunderstorm
in three nights lightninged your face
the curves of your body at me
again so healthy it was
all I could do not to take that arm
and work my way inland

                         but now it's morning
your stomach's a riot and I'm offering
slices of cool orange melon, a bright
yellow banana, the pop in your mouth
of sweet green grapes and the raspberry
tips of your breasts sway before me
as you lean at me again begging
with an outstretched cup
for a bit more tea, I feel
all that makes the man in me
race round my wide-awake
healthy body like bees in a yard
but all that makes the decent man
in me pours your tea, averts

my glad eyes again, promising myself,
with your healthy compliance,
the eager taste of those
tart red fruits the moment your
bees start buzzing again.

Why We Fought

We fought because Princess Diana
died and there wasn't a single way
not to know about it. We heard
from our Native guide as we got into the boat
last day of August with a cooler
half-full of fish and as far from news
as we could get, but he had a satellite
dish. He grinned as he told us.
I said later it was the sun in his eyes.
You said he was shy, didn't know how
we'd take the news.

We fought because two days of news
coverage wore me down. I said Jesus
wasn't good enough anymore. Or Mohammed.
We had to have Elvis and now Diana.
How did the photographers know
she'd be in Paris? Her own people sold tips
to the press. No one has any honour anymore.

We fought because your youngest brother
died the same day as Diana, fourteen
years ago. He was born the same year.
His death was just as senseless and sordid.
Someone was drunk there, too.

We fought because you said you liked
Diana. That she was more
than just a newspaper star. I didn't say
anything. Later I said something stupid.
Or perhaps unkind. Then
something else.

We fought because we had never understood
who this young woman was, but felt
badly that she died with men taking
pictures of her dying. We weren't sure
how to take all this news.

We fought.

Being Married

Leaf-roller bugs have blighted the green ash
I planted last fall while you were
in Victoria nursing a friend with cancer.
It's been raining for three days and
when I looked today, the leaves were curled
and black. I phoned and got advice, then
poured poison into the ground. Over the phone
you asked if I wore gloves, if I breathed
the fumes. I'm beside myself. You've
been away five weeks. I make it sound
as if you're always away, but that's not
it at all. Just now you're gone and the garden
rushes me every time I step out the door.
Leaf-roller bugs. Who'd have thought of it?
The man at the store says whoever sold me
the tree should have told me. I tell him
this is the only tree I've ever planted.
The only house I've ever owned. The only
care I've really taken with every plant
that surrounds it, every creak it makes
inside. It's just a house, after all.
It could burn down.

Not tonight it won't.
I've checked. I've picked all the black
leaves off the tree. All I could reach.
I read the instructions on the poison
after I called you. I've washed
carefully now. I may call you again
just to let you know.

Smoking

Her breasts shine out at me
from either side of her shirt slashed
open to below the band of black lace
that holds them in the white sky
of her chest. We've just left
the Broadway Theatre, she,
her friend and me, two actresses
from the UK talking over the play,
how an actress must live
inside her character, inhabit
every silence, the moon,
our fat prairie moon, the same one
they've got in London and vivid
across the moors, glowing above and yes
I say, my wife's away
another week, speak knowledgeably
of the theatre, of two poets
they used to see lurking about
their library back home in Hull,
each of these women's faces
surely that of some famous
goddess, perhaps a minor one, the slight
cleft in this one's chin, the full
softness of the other one's cheeks,
and her breasts at which, I admit,
I continue to sneak quick peeks, always
as if I'm just turning to survey
the crowd in the street, that moon
full of itself in our dark sky, black
as that band of lace across her chest,
as Orion's belt on the other woman's dress
from which she removes that familiar

red pack and I say yes
I've quit and my wife's away
and how I long to touch
– just now – that piece of lace but
instead I say   yes, yes,
I could really use
that proferred cigarette.

Father Alone

Pulling away from the Tsawwassen docks
I spot purple starfish stuck to the pilings
the same kind I told you
I brought home as a kid
thinking they'd dry out in no time
then I'd display them in my room.

You were thirteen when I told you
how your grandpa couldn't figure out
where the hellish stink was coming from,
finally found the funky starfish
under the porch,
asked me what I was thinking.

Now that was a good story, lots
of stink and father annoyed.

I think I wish you were here now
to show you the starfish, remind you
of my story, but you're fifteen
and would merely nod. Yeah,
starfish, as this big boat full of people,
some your age, and magazines,
video machines, pulls out for Victoria,
where you lived a year with your mother.
There's not a thing there I can show you,
nothing you haven't seen better.

I'm alone. Four days on the road
to meet up with the new
woman in my life. Motels and restaurants
by myself. I want you here
when you were five. The kindergarten
teacher hadn't told us you couldn't

keep up with the others then.
You hadn't been teased then. We all thought
we had a working family then. I still
kick myself for tearing it all apart,
know its inevitability, that it wasn't
all about me. But lonely like this
I'm ready to take all the blame,
pull you to my side when you were still
small enough never to question
why I'd suddenly hug you in sheer wonder
that I had something to do with
making someone like you. Point
to the purple starfish, look at them
in those purple clumps, I'd say,
and you the most fascinated audience
I've ever had.

Slow Boat

Six weeks apart and I'm an hour
away from you, the ferry rocking
me across the strait, the seals, the blast
of the horn through Active Pass. Each time
I've imagined our meeting I've been
too rattled to drive, to think, plugging in
tape after tape down the rainy Fraser Canyon. Call it
deep desire, or a crasser word, I know
the only way to get to you safely
is to concentrate on the view, the cameras,
the binoculars, so many people talking
the way that woman – is she getting
him another coffee – rises
to the caress of her man.

Winter Mouths

Despite the hot summer myth
the bodies creamed with sweat
and lathered into the Legion Hall
to dance the sweet row-day-o
this country's name is really
winter.

It's cold that makes us move:
September football fires us
October Hallowe'en makes us face
the faces we've always wanted
as we eat our kids' candy
through grey November
all the schedules all the parties
winding faster into winter.

My school dates always wore fake fur
their pink frosted lips such
a startling contrast they kissed me
in backdoor forty below and couldn't
ask me in. They weren't old
enough. Now we kiss on doorsteps
northern lights exploding over both
our closed colourful eyes, our winter
mouths pressed warm together.

Coming back from the high school gym, I say
hey basketball mom, let's kiss
then go in
and get warmer.

Polka Suicide

The annual Ballroom Dancing Soiree is all waltzes
foxtrots and rhumbas, a few cha chas, sambas
and the West Coast swing. Once only on the evening's
card, the old-fashioned polka that usually clears
the floor. For all our big-city leanings this is
Saskatchewan after all.
                                    I'm pushing forty-five,
my wife and I stick to the gentler numbers till I hear
the hee-haw pant of that crazy accordion, the Norwegian
Steinway, the Ukrainian Philharmonic, then I'm on my feet
and running for the floor. My wife's too sensible for
these shenanigans, she'd prefer to watch me grab
some teenage bundle of fuzzy twigs who screams
her delight when her feet leave the boards. I'd tell her,
honey, any man could lift a woman with as little
heft as you but I've got no wind, feel every walk I wish
I'd taken to the store for smokes.
                                    Better to get a woman
my age with as little sense as me, I feel her flesh
crowding her undergarments for space, her hot breath
crashing into my face as we grin fiercely through
our desperate need for oxygen, for stronger knees.

That night in bed she turns to her husband, the fire
in her lungs now a steady thrum between the legs
my right thigh slammed repeatedly, I'm just not
the dancer I used to be. Lying in my own bed,
my wife content beside me having been left alone
to fall fast asleep, every part of me aches as it
rattles back down to the man my body's
forced me to be.

Home Dye Job

I remember when I first knew
you were coming. I stood in a field,
a shortcut to the local store, staring
at the 401 a mile off, the big trucks
gunning past Kingston, everyone I knew
many miles distant and us with a kid
on the way. You scared me then, though
I learned to hold you not
as if you would break, though you did, your head
on the Franklin heater, on the swing, the sight
of you in Intensive Care crying for us
after you'd inhaled the Macadamia nut
we slapped ourselves for letting you have.

The usual round of cuts and bangs then
the whap whap whap of your head
against the backseat amid the fishing tackle,
your eyes rolled back and me screaming
at Rod to pull the car over. Then round
after round of pictures of your brain,
assuring you nothing's changed, when
it has. You can still play football, bang
heads, this one I hold like it won't
break, when it has and still can because
it's different, but the same head I've held
dear to my chest though less frequently
now you tower over me, bent now
into the sink where I rinse out the dye
you've changed yourself with.

                        You know
I could have looked at you as yourself
for ages, know the time is running short
I can hold you at all, grinning up at me

with your new hair, believing, though
you swear it isn't so, that this colour
will change your life. Me, with my hands
still holding you, knowing that it's just
one more thing that will do exactly that,
change you into something older and farther
away from me, though I'm gloriously happy
you still ask me to help.

Cleaning

I sit quietly examining
my hands, these rude red marks
on my right fingers are
what the pike gave me
for ripping out his gills
after I slit his belly, your nephew's
first fish, his eyes the size
of the moon above that chopped
the water into little cups of gold
spilling against my legs
where I stood up to the dock and pulled
out the intestines, the tiny
heart the boy was so eager
to see, I chucked the lot
into tall cattails
for the muskrat watching
from ten feet offshore
telling the boy he did well,
he did very well, telling him muskrat
and moon, telling him stars
and the clouds moving up
the northern horizon, how
we were lucky, that tomorrow
would be a hard rain, my fingers
bleeding and the pike's liver
squirming up under my thumb
the boy so impressed
with what he'd done, how much there was
left to do, catch a fish
and clean it, this fatherless boy
standing in the dark moon-cut
water with this man his aunt
brought along, telling the boy
he did well, and the next day

phoning my own son
to tell him this fish wasn't
as big as the one he caught
telling him I'd see him soon
that there was plenty of luck
left in the lake
my hands red and sore and ready
as I hung up the phone.

Becoming Dad

To make a fire seems the whole point
of coming to the lake, the fishing,
swimming, canoeing, great gallons
of Coke and Seven-Up are great,
but to build a fire and show me
what he's learned at camp, this seems
the height of manhood for my son,
bending to the task now he's tossed aside
the axe I was a little worried
he'd take his foot off with. The cooking fire
he calls it, not to be confused with other
lesser fires for sheer amusement,
the wood stacked just so and a minimum
of paper – he's proud to show me – just
the bare few folds to get it going
then a blaze we could forge with
to roast our four wieners, his smile
wide with mustard, the ketchup
he's spilled down his shirt and shorts,
then he's off with his rod and tackle,
a chunk of wood he's cut to brain
whatever fish he gets. I sit here
at the table three hours later staring
at the pile of ash and two remnants
of wood that did not burn, a ghost
of smoke leaking from the one,
both alone and unimportant now
he's showed me he's got what it takes
to be a man, become the dad.

The Christmas Question

Scrubbing the house for our big Christmas
party, we've already turned it into the biggest
Christmas cliché, the happy couple who
fight their way through the vacuuming, the placing
of holly, hiding the little piles of things we've
lived with through the fall as they prompt
an almost festive savagery of muttering and
outright swearing. I'd threaten to phone
all our guests, call the whole thing off like
that other couple I told you about years ago,
except I'd probably forget someone, poor
bastard, here alone at nine o'clock, his Black
Magic chocolates under a red bow and smiling
faintly as we turn off the TV, bring him in
so he can excuse his way out again.
                                        No, I wouldn't
dare give some of our friends the best Christmas
gift I could give 'em, the satisfaction of saying
to one another when they gather elsewhere –
the babysitters in place anyway – that all the
public loving we've done, arm-in-arm stuff,
laughing at the theatre, gazing at one another
in cafés, was all a sham, easy to keep up
for a few years, but that some little thing,
some inevitable Christmas cleaning, finally
tore it all down.

No. They're wrong. The Christmas party
goes on. Even if we're still angry at eight
we'll bring them in with a smile, fake it
till we spot one another across the smoked rainbow
trout around eleven, the forgiveness light
in our eyes from all those fucking candles
you insisted I buy, or you buy, lighting

the room, our room, our friends envying
us our ease with one another, each of them
saying in wonder, how do you still speak
to one another after getting ready
for one of these things?

This Year's Theme

New Year's Eve for us is usually
home and in bed by eleven, but
this year it's a Polyester party,
dragging out those hideous checks
and colours from 1972 in which I'm
memorialized in a number of wedding albums
throughout Southwest Saskatchewan but
those clothes are gone now and we've repaired
to the Mennonite Clothes Closet
and Sally Ann to refurbish as raffishly
as possible, giggling as we discuss
our wardrobe, and your daughter
and her friends wonder just how old
you have to be before you start
having theme parties, is it a forties thing?

We tell them we were having
theme parties at their age, gala events,
and they politely suffer another droll meandering
through our ditzy past: yes, I say
at every one was the constant theme
of drunkenness and much marijuana,
loud music and all of us hollering
brave stories at one another
about when we'd go to Tangiers or
Calgary, then someone would puke
on someone's mother's vanity, just like
they did at the last party and
the party before, and some guy would be
in the bedroom with someone's girlfriend,
not his, then there's the fight, the tears,
and all that wonderful talking
about what happened and who
did what to who first.

Were these not bold themes? we ask:
Love, Jealousy, Retribution, Talking
their way into little legends and
the young women don't answer but
file downstairs to change and phone
and find out who's picking who up
and just who was that guy last night
anyway.

Savoy

She won't let me cook
the cabbage I just bought
at the farmers' market
from the old woman
who grows them specially

Says it's too perfect
each ruffled light green
leaf layering gently over
each ruffled light green leaf

She places it squarely
in the middle of our table
in a bowl she bought
last summer and it soothes
the hearts of all who enter

her brothers, their wives and
noisy children, her children, mine,
all our friends, they look
and laugh, then linger, almost
touching with the tips
of their fingers the ruffled
leaves that lace together,
then quietly they leave the room

to us, standing staring
at the green lightly lingering
in its leaves, holding each leaf
gently together on our table

Acknowledgements

Some of these poems have appeared in various issues of *Grain* magazine. "Winter Kiss" was written for a winter celebration organized by Paula Patola at Aden Bowman Collegiate Institute in Saskatoon.

The author wishes to thank the Saskatchewan Arts Board for a grant during the writing of this book and the Saskatchewan Writers' Guild for time at its winter writers' colonies, St. Peter's Abbey, Muenster, Saskatchewan. Thanks to the staff at St. Peter's Abbey. Thanks to Geoffrey Ursell for his editorial guidance, and to Betsy Warland, Edna Alford, and Elizabeth Philips for strong suggestions during the editorial process. Much appreciated. Thanks also to Jared Fedorchuk for invaluable technical assistance. Many thanks through the years to Lois Simmie, Ray Stephanson, Dr. B., Lisa S., Hoe Mark, Don Barss, Donna Wilson, Howard Derksen, Dave Carpenter and Honor Kever, Half-Century, Good Morning Group, Ward Wilson, Colleen Fitzgerald, Ruth and Stewart Robertson, Elizabeth Smith and Janet Larson and their families, the Maxwell family, and to the memory of their dear father, Grant. Also to the memory of Anne Szumigalski. Warm thanks to Mary Maxwell, first reader.

Photo: Mary Maxwell

About the Author

William Robertson is the author of three previous poetry collections – *Somewhere Else, Standing on Our Own Two Feet,* and *Adult Language Warning* – the first two of these also published by Coteau Books. His work has been widely published in literary magazines and anthologies. He teaches English at several institutions, and has led writing workshops at Sage Hill Writing Experience and others.

Born in Tokyo, Japan, William Robertson lived in several Japanese cities, in Ontario, and on the Canadian West Coast by the time he was twelve. He spent his teen years in Shaunavon, Sask, before heading to Saskatoon to obtain an MA in English from the University of Saskatchewan. He continues to live in Saskatoon.